W9-ARF-103

An Insider's Guide to

FIELD HOCKEY

ABIGAEL MCINTYRE AND HELEN CONNOLLY

rosen publishing's
rosen central®

NEW YORK

Published in 2015 by The Rosen Publishing Group, Inc.
29 East 21st Street, New York, NY 10010

First Edition

Library of Congress Cataloging-in-Publication Data

McIntyre, Abigael.
An insider's guide to field hockey/Abigael McIntyre and Helen Connolly.
   pages cm.—(Sports tips, techniques, and strategies)
Includes bibliographical references and index.
ISBN 978-1-4777-8073-2 (library bound)
ISBN 978-1-4777-8074-9 (pbk.)
ISBN 978-1-4777-8075-6 (6-pack)
1. Field hockey—Juvenile literature. I. Title.

GV1017.H7M45 2015
796.355—dc23

2014013699

Manufactured in Malaysia

Metric Conversion Chart			
1 inch	2.54 centimeters 25.4 millimeters	1 cup	250 milliliters
1 foot	30.48 centimeters	1 ounce	28 grams
1 yard	.914 meters	1 fluid ounce	30 milliliters
1 square foot	.093 square meters	1 teaspoon	5 milliliters
1 square mile	2.59 square kilometers	1 tablespoon	15 milliliters
1 ton	.907 metric tons	1 quart	.946 liters
1 pound	454 grams	355 degrees F	180 degrees C
1 mile	1.609 kilometers		

Contents

CHAPTER 1

A History of Field Hockey

Humans have been playing ball-and-stick games similar to modern field hockey since ancient times. While no one can say exactly when or where the game was invented, evidence of its existence in ancient cultures abounds. Four-thousand-year-old drawings of men playing a form of field hockey have been found in

This tablet at the National Archaeological Museum of Athens, dating back to 500 BCE, shows people playing a form of field hockey.

tombs in Egypt. Over the centuries, different versions of the sport were played by the Arabs, Aztecs, Ethiopians, Greeks, Persians, and Romans. Field hockey is connected to other established games such as the French game *hocquet,* from which sport historians believe the term "hockey" may have been derived. But the sport we know as hockey today originated in England in the mid-1800s.

This 1646 drawing shows Mapuche Indians of modern-day Chile playing "palín," a game similar to field hockey.

Though men's hockey originated in England, it is now popular throughout the world.

Hockey Clubs

The first men's hockey club, Blackheath, was formed in southeast London in 1849. A field hockey club is like a league with several teams and is organized by region. However, it was another hockey club in London, Teddington, that helped refine and modernize the game. Teddington developed certain conventions, such as the use of the shooting circle — the area of the field that a player must be in to score a goal — and the banning of lifting sticks above the shoulder. Thirty-seven years later, in 1886, the Hockey Association was founded in London.

Hockey Catches Women's Fancy

While men's field hockey clubs were gaining in popularity, the heavy ball and thick sticks that were used could potentially hurt a person, so in those times the game was considered too dangerous for women to play. However, as leisure activities like croquet, another ball-and-stick sport, became socially acceptable for women to play, the equipment used in field hockey didn't seem as threatening. Physical activity was difficult for women in the Victorian era because of the heavy layers of clothing and ankle-length dresses they were expected to wear. It was difficult to move, let alone run, in such apparel. In spite of that, women did take up the sport. In fact,

Kilts and athletic shorts have replaced the Victorian-era dresses once worn by female field hockey players

today field hockey is one of the few sports in which women wear a skirt on the field, since most women's field hockey uniforms include a kilt.

Hockey Goes Global

As field hockey gained popularity with women, it became the first sport that was deemed proper for them to play. In 1887, the first women's hockey club was created in East Mosley in northern England. Two years later, the All England Women's Hockey Association was founded.

Scotland scores against Germany in the 1908 Summer Olympics held in London, United Kingdom.

As field hockey became a favorite pastime among both sexes in England, its popularity began to spread around the world. The British army introduced the game in the late 1800s to India. This subsequently led to the first international competition in 1895. In 1908, men's field hockey was approved as an Olympic sport and was played at the Olympic Games in London that year.

Hockey Reaches the U.S.A.

Eventually, field hockey spread to the United States, pretty much as a result of the efforts of a twenty-eight-year-old English woman named Constance Applebee. Applebee was a physical education teacher who was attending a seminar at Harvard University in Massachusetts in the summer of 1901.

She was alarmed and horrified by the lack of exercise she observed in young American women, so she put together an impromptu hockey exhibition behind the Harvard gymnasium. Because of the enthusiastic response to the game at Harvard, Applebee began to travel around to the most prestigious women's colleges in the Northeast, starting up field hockey teams at Vassar, Wellesley, Smith, Radcliffe, Mount Holyoke, and Bryn Mawr. Later that same year, the American Field Hockey Association, an organization for women players, was founded in Philadelphia, and Constance Applebee was elected president.

Constance Applebee demonstrates field hockey positions in 1903.

The Victorian era imposed a lot of restrictions on women in terms of clothing, behavior, and lifestyle. Women were expected to obey men, and were not expected to be outspoken or playful. Athletic activity that went beyond parlor games was unacceptable. By the turn of the century, however, women began to agitate for equality in politics, in the workplace, and in social relations. When Constance Applebee arrived in America in 1901 to teach young female college students the game of field hockey, the suffrage movement was in full swing. Women wanted the same basic rights as men; they wanted to develop mentally and physically as individuals. Increased enrollment in women's colleges and interest in field hockey reflected these desires. Because of Applebee's efforts during field hockey's early stages in America, it became known mostly as a women's sport in the United States.

In 1920, a U.S. women's touring team began to compete internationally. Three years later Constance Applebee opened the first field hockey camp,

The women's hockey team from Zimbabwe celebrates after winning the 1980 Olympic Gold.

Tegawitha, in the Pocono Mountains of Pennsylvania. Girls went to Camp Tegawitha to increase their skills and to meet other women who enjoyed the game. They exercised and ran practice drills by day and studied the theory of the sport by night. The camp remained successful for decades and eventually grew to encompass a variety of athletic activities for women, until the camp closed at the end of the 20th century. Applebee continued to play an important role in pioneering this burgeoning competitive sport for women in the United States until she retired in 1971, at the age of 97. After her retirement, Applebee moved back to England, where she lived until her death at the age of 107!

The Shape of the Ball

The Blackheath field hockey club played with a solid cube of black rubber for the "ball." The use of the a spherical ball was eventually introduced by Teddington.

The shape of the hockey ball has evolved from early games. Today, official balls are dimpled, like a golf ball.

Men's Field Hockey

Though men's field hockey did not catch on in the United States the way women's field hockey did, the sport is played by men. The first recorded men's game wasn't played until 1928 in Pennsylvania. Later that year, the Field Hockey Association of America (FHAA), an organization for men's field hockey, was founded. In 1930, the FHAA became a member of the Fédération Internationale de Hockey (FIH), hockey's international federation. An American named Henry Greer, who many consider the founder of men's hockey in the United States, was president of the FHAA from 1930 to 1959. Greer coached and played on the U.S. men's team in its first Olympic Games in Los Angeles in 1932. It took home the bronze medal that year, losing to Japan, who took silver, and India, who took gold.

The U.S. team plays against the Indian team at the
Los Angeles Summer Olympics in 1932.

Women's Field Hockey Competition

Although the sport had been played by women since its inception, women's field hockey didn't receive recognition for serious international competition until 1975, when the first Women's World Cup was held. In 1980, women's field hockey was added to the Olympic program. That year, the Olympics were held in Moscow in what was then the Soviet Union. Due to the political climate of the Cold War, the United States was not friendly with the Soviet Union.

The United States, along with sixty-one other countries, decided to boycott the 1980 Olympic Games. It wasn't until the 1984 Olympic Games in Los Angeles that the U.S. women's field hockey team actually got to compete. It took home the bronze medal that year.

Women's hockey is very popular in the United States today. Here, two university teams compete against each other.

The United States Field Hockey Association (USFHA)

The FHAA and the United States Field Hockey Association (USFHA) merged to form one national organization for both women's and men's field hockey in 1993, at the request of the United States Olympic Committee (USOC). They retained the name of USFHA. With more than 15,000 members, the USFHA is a very active organization. It is a member of the USOC, the Pan American Hockey Federation (PAFH), and the FIH. The USFHA still promotes the sport of field hockey and prepares teams to participate in international games, including the Olympics.

Today, field hockey is enjoyed by millions of men and women, and the FIH consists of 127 member associations spread over all six inhabited continents. Its popularity continues to grow, with new clubs and teams, both amateur and professional, sprouting up all over. Apart from soccer, it is the largest team sport in the world.

CHAPTER 2

What You Need

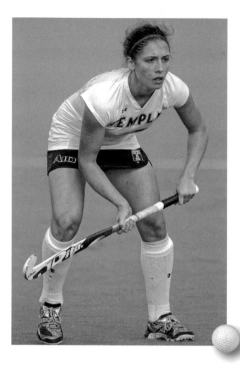

The Ball

Cricket, a bat-and-ball game similar to modern baseball, had already been embraced as an English pastime around the time that field hockey was gaining momentum in the late 1800s. At first, it was natural for field hockey enthusiasts to use leather-covered cricket balls, but today the field hockey ball is very different. It is completely constructed out of polyvinyl chloride (PVC), which is a type of hard plastic. The plastic ball proved to be better for outdoor games, as it does not absorb any moisture. It is also built to withstand the heat of friction and the frequent impacts of bouncing. The ball is slightly larger than a baseball, measuring about 9 inches in circumference and weighing about 5.5 ounces. Younger players are permitted to play with a lighter ball. An official game ball is dimpled like a golf ball, but practice balls are not required to be. For international games, the ball color must be white, but for other games the ball can be any color, just so long as it contrasts with the color of the field for better visibility. The ball can reach speeds of up to 100 miles per hour when hit with a field hockey stick.

Hockey players, like cricket players, wear pads for protection.

Protective Gear

A field hockey ball, because of its speed, weight, and texture, could potentially cause serious injury to a player if it makes contact with an unprotected area of the body. This is why players are required to wear shin guards and mouth guards. Hockey shin guards are made from lightweight plastic or foam and are crucial in protecting players' legs from speeding balls and heavy, swinging sticks. Because of the protection that shin guards provide, players have the confidence to play more aggressively, which in turn, improves their game.

When women's field hockey was first founded in America, players were required to wear a modest and cumbersome ensemble that included long-sleeved flannel shirts and corduroy skirts that fell several inches below the knee. Thankfully, the field hockey uniforms that women wear today, consisting of a short-sleeved shirt and a kilt, are much more comfortable.

A women's hockey team poses for a photograph in 1925. Long skirts were customary while playing in those days.

The protective gear for goalies is extensive as the ball
is potentially dangerous if it hits the goalie in an unprotected area.

The Uniform

To protect their legs when diving for balls, many women wear shorts similar to bicycle shorts. Men's and children's field hockey uniforms are virtually the same, except that men wear shorts instead of kilts. Members of the same team are required to wear matching uniforms and the same color knee socks. Shirts are required to have a number printed on the front and back so that the referees can identify each player.

Because of the amount of running involved in field hockey and the importance that is placed on quickness and agility, footwear with proper support is essential. For outdoor grass fields, leather or nylon cleats are needed for traction. For indoor games with a flat AstroTurf field, flat-soled running shoes are suitable.

Female hockey players wear skirts or shorts while playing. The color of their uniform is determined by the team they play for.

Both men and women goalkeepers wear shorts and a shirt that differ in color from that of their team and the opponent's team. Goalies are required to cover nearly their whole body with protective gear that will shield them from serious injury, while at the same time allowing for mobility. Field hockey goalies wear helmets with face masks, similar to those of ice hockey goalies. They also wear a throat guard, a chest pad, shoulder pads, elbow pads, an abdominal guard, padded overall pants with a pelvic guard, leg pads, large gloves with padded knuckles, and "kickers" for the feet and ankles. Kickers, worn over shoes, are lightweight boots that are used to kick the ball out of the striking circle.

The Hockey Stick

A player's most important piece of equipment, apart from protective gear, is his or her stick. Field hockey sticks are used to handle the ball on the field. The sticks have a straight handle and shaft and a curved head. They are made of wood, are about three feet long, and must weigh between twelve and twenty-eight ounces. It is important for a player to take into account his or her own height and strength when picking a stick size that would best suit him or her and enhance performance on the field. A common way to choose the proper stick length is to place the head of the stick on the ground next to the leg. The handle of the stick should come up to the top of a player's hip. All sticks must be able to pass through a two-inch ring, from the head to the handle. If a stick cannot pass through such a ring, it cannot be used in a game.

The ball can only be hit with the front, or flat half, of the stick. The design of the stick has changed over the years, but today the two most important features of a stick are its reinforcement and the shape of the head. The stiffer a field hockey stick, the harder it will hit the ball. Reinforcements are important in making the stick stronger and improving a player's game. There are some materials that can be added to a basic wooden shaft and handle in order to make it stronger. Fiberglass will add strength and will lengthen the life span of a stick. Both Kevlar and Dyneema will increase shock absorbency while carbon will add stiffness. A player attempts to pick a stick made of materials that will enhance his or her skills or style of playing.

Though hockey sticks have the same basic shape, the shape of the head differs depending on the player's position.

Regardless of the player's size, the curved head of the stick cannot be larger than four inches or be made of any material other than wood. Sharp edges are not permitted. Instead, the edges must be completely rounded. The three main head shapes are the shorti, the midi, and the hook. The shorti is the traditional head shape and is preferred by many players for the extra dexterity it affords. Because shorti heads are carved from one piece of wood, they are stronger and longer lasting, and they have a more centered "sweet spot" for striking. Midi and hook heads are made of several pieces of wood that are laminated together. They aren't as strong or durable as shorti heads, but as long as a player takes proper care of his or her stick, midi and hook heads can be used for a considerable amount of time. Midi and hook heads are advantageous for dribbling and flicking (when a player snaps his or her wrist to lift the ball in the air for quick passes or shots).

The length and shape of the shaft also differ depending on the position of the player.

The shafts of the sticks can also come in different shapes. While straight shafts are more common, some players, particularly goalies, prefer a kinked shaft. A kinked shaft can stop a ball better than a straight stick when it is laid on its side, offering a larger save area to the goalie.

The left hand is placed on top of the stick, aligned with the flat side of the stick. The right hand is stretched out five to seven inches below it.

Holding the Stick

It's important for a player to learn how to hold the stick properly once he or she has chosen the proper stick to optimize his or her game. When someone picks up a field hockey stick for the first time, his or her first instinct might be to hold it like one would hold a baseball bat. However, the proper way to hold a stick is called the "shake hands grip." It is achieved by reaching out the left hand as if to shake someone's hand and grabbing the top of the handle of the stick, so the flat side is aligned with the palm of the left hand. Then reach out with the right hand, as if to shake someone's hand, and place it about five to seven inches below the left hand.

The correct way to grip a hockey stick is, as shown above, with the right hand below the left.

The stick should be held pointing forward, with the flat side facing the left and the toe pointing up. It should be held comfortably away from the player's body. The left hand controls the stick's movement, while the right hand serves as a guide.

Reverse Grip

Because the ball can only be hit with the flat side of the stick, it must be hit a different way when the ball is on the player's left side. The "reverse grip" is used for this purpose. It is achieved by loosening the grip of the right hand and turning the left hand until the inside of the left wrist is facing up. The flat side faces to the right with the toe pointing toward the player. Once the transition is made from shake hands to reverse grip, the right-hand grip should tighten. It is important for a player to retain a firm grip on the stick with his or her fingers together. There is a greater chance of injury caused by stray sticks and balls if the player's fingers separate.

This player (in green) gets ready to hold the stick in the reverse position to gain control of the ball.

CHAPTER 3

The Game

The actual fun and excitement of playing the game on the field begins only after a player has the essential equipment. Field hockey is often played outdoors on the grass, but more serious competitions take place indoors on a completely flat AstroTurf surface, where the players and the ball can move faster. Whether the game is played indoors or out, the size and markings of the field remain the same.

The Field

The standard size of a hockey field is rectangular, measuring sixty yards wide by 100 yards long. The field is divided into two halves by the center line. Each half of the field is then divided by a twenty-five-yard line. All lines on the field must be three inches wide. The end line, the goal line (the part of the end line between the goal posts), and the sidelines are all part of the field of play. This means that in order for a ball to be out of bounds or for a goal to be scored, the ball must completely pass over any of those lines.

In each corner of the field, a flag is placed at the outer edge of the line. A flag is also placed at each twenty-five-yard line, one yard outside the sidelines. The flags assist the referee on where to award a free hit to the offense when the defense commits a foul within its twenty-five-yard area. There are six lines, measuring two yards in length, that are placed across the center line and five yards away from and parallel to each sideline. The purpose of these lines is to assist in determining where sideline hits should be taken after a ball is knocked out of bounds. Twelve-inch-long lines are placed sixteen yards away from and parallel to the end line. Other twelve-inch lines, penalty corner hit marks, are placed inside the field on the end lines at five- and ten-yard intervals, measured from the sides of the goalposts. Finally, placed seven yards from the center of the goal line is the penalty spot, where the ball is placed to take a penalty shot.

5 yard

25 yard

penalty corner
defender's mark

4 yard

25-yard line

centre line

25-yard line

5 yard

shooting circle

penalty shots

goal

16 yard

7 yard

5 yard

penalty corner
attacker's mark

HYUNDAI ThyssenKrupp WEBER WEBER WEBER Sparkasse Duisburg

24

Sparkasse
Duisburg

Professional hockey matches are played indoors. The diagram
above specifies the dimensions of the field.

This player gets ready to take a shot from inside the shooting circle.

The Striking Circle

The striking circle, or shooting circle, is usually a semicircle. The ends are sixteen yards from each goal post, creating an area that extends sixteen yards into the field, with a four-yard straight line parallel to the goal line. The object of the game is to shoot the ball in the opponent's goal for one point. The team with the most points at the end of a game wins. A score can only be made by a shot taken from within the striking circle. The ball must pass completely over the goal line in order for a score to count. Additionally, the ball cannot be lifted or flicked into the circle, but must be brought or passed in on the ground.

The Goal

At each end of the field is a goal cage constructed out of two goalposts, a horizontal crossbar, a backboard, and sideboards, with a net covering the top and sides. The goal cage, like the field, is

A hockey goal is twelve feet wide and seven feet high.

rectangular, measuring twelve feet wide and seven feet high. The posts and crossbar are painted white, while the backboard is painted dark and measures eighteen inches high. The sideboards also measure eighteen inches high and are four feet wide, which determines the depth of the goal area.

The Captain

Each team has a captain on the field at all times who wears an armband to distinguish him or herself from the other players. The team captains have four responsibilities during a competitive game. Before the game begins, the captains meet the referees for a coin toss to determine which end of the field they'll defend and who will have possession of the ball for the opening pass. The captains are also in charge of executing player substitutions and identifying the goalie. If the captain is ever suspended or needs to be replaced, it is his or her duty to appoint a new captain. Finally, it is the captain's responsibility to make sure that his or her teammates behave properly, are respectful of the game's rules, and exhibit good sportsmanship.

The Referee

In field hockey, there are two referees, one for each half of the field. The referees enforce the rules and make sure the game is played fairly. They are positioned on the sidelines and only enter the field when necessary. Each referee is responsible only for his or her half of the field and is in charge of deciding when a ball is knocked out of bounds, when to award a team with a penalty shot or a free hit, and calling violations on players.

The referee must be quick and able to spot fouls efficiently.

How It's Played

The game consists of two halves that are between twenty-five and thirty-five minutes long, depending on the league, with a halftime break that is around ten minutes long. Each half is played continuously, although sometimes two sixty-second time-outs are

No player is allowed to touch the ball with their hands, or any other part of their body, except for the goalkeeper.

allotted to each team. After halftime, the teams switch sides of the field and swap goals, so that there are no unfair advantages due to the makeup of the field. The beginning of each half of the game is started with a "passback" at the center of the field, after the referee has blown his or her whistle. A player must pass the ball to a teammate who is at least 3.3 feet behind him or her. Passbacks are also used after an opposing team has scored a goal.

Much like soccer players, field hockey players are not allowed to use their hands to touch the ball. The rules specify that players may only use their sticks when handling the ball, except for the goalie, who is permitted to use any part of his or her body to prevent a goal. The goalie is also allowed to kick the ball, but only when he or she is inside the striking circle. If a goalie is outside of the striking circle, the same stick-only rule applies to him or her as it does for the rest of the team.

Some Common Strategies

The most common move in field hockey is a "drive." A drive is when a player applies a hard backswing to the ball, with both hands together at the top of the stick. It is used on passes and shots on the goal. When the curve of the stick is used to scoop up the ball over an opponents stick, it is called a "scoop."

A "push pass" is the most accurate pass. It is a quick stroke with the wrist. A "slap shot" is the most powerful stroke in field hockey. It is a hard shot on the goal, executed with a half backswing and hands slightly apart on the stick. The motions of many field hockey strokes are similar to that of a golf swing. However, when playing the ball in field hockey, raising the stick above the shoulder is considered a dangerous use of the stick, and a foul will be called.

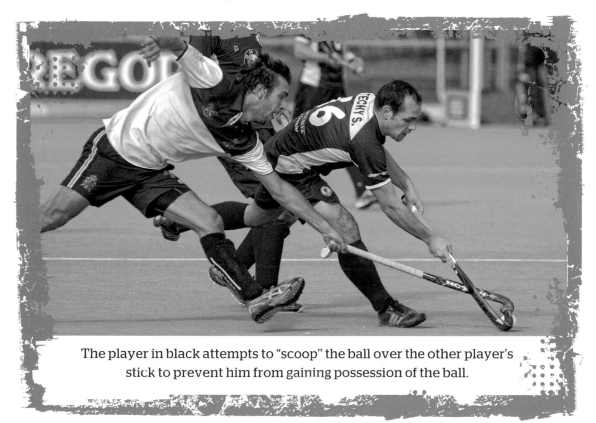

The player in black attempts to "scoop" the ball over the other player's stick to prevent him from gaining possession of the ball.

A color-coded card system is used to distinguish the severity of an infraction or penalty. Green cards are issued by the referee as a warning for minor violations. Yellow cards are issued by the referee for an intentional foul, such as rough play. A player who receives a yellow card is suspended from the game for five minutes. The team must play one member short during that time. Red cards are issued for serious intentional fouls such as deliberate body contact or verbal abuse. A player is ejected from the game and suspended from the team's next game if he or she receives a red card.

Fouls

Rule violations and fouls are often committed and called on players for many possible reasons. An "obstruction" is called against a player who uses his or her stick, shoulder, or body as a barrier. While shielding the ball with one's body is part of the game strategy in most sports, it is not allowed in field hockey, where each player is supposed to have an equal chance at the ball as it is played up and down the field. Instead of using obstruction as a means to gain control of the ball, players are allowed to "jab," which means continual poking at the ball to make the opponent lose possession.

"Back stick" is called when a player uses the round (back) side of the hockey stick to play the ball. "Undercutting" is called when a player chops at the ball with his or her stick, to lift it in an unsafe manner. "Hooking" is called when a player uses the curved head of his or her stick to hook an opponent's stick. "Advancing" is called when a player pushes or moves the ball in any way other than with his or her stick. When a foul is called on a player, a free hit from a penalty corner is awarded to the opposing team.

Two players vie for the ball during a game. Though blocking the ball with one's body is not permitted, players are allowed to "jab" at the ball, as shown above.

Free Hits and Penalty Corners

Most scoring opportunities in field hockey come from free hits and hits from penalty corners (also known as short corners). A free hit is awarded on any violation that takes place outside the striking circle and takes place at the location of the foul. All opposing players must stand at a minimum distance of five yards from where the hit is taken. Most free hits are taken

Argentinian player Lopez (in orange) commits a foul on Dutch player Kemperman, which requires a penalty corner shot, during the 2014 Argentina – Netherlands World Cup Hockey game.

as a push pass, scoop, flick, or drive. A hit from a penalty corner is awarded to the offense when the defensive team commits a foul inside the striking circle or intentionally hits the ball out of bounds. The penalty corner shot is taken from a point on the goal line, at least ten yards away from the goal. The rest of the offense must stand with their feet and sticks outside of the striking circle, while four defense players and their goalie stand behind the end line.

Penalty Stroke

A penalty stroke is a little bit different from a hit from a penalty corner. A penalty stroke is awarded to the offense when a referee concludes that a defensive violation hampered a sure goal. An offensive player then goes one-on-one with the goalie and is given five seconds to shoot. All other players must remain behind the twenty-five-yard line. A sixteen-yard hit is awarded to the defense when the offense sends the ball over the end line or commits a violation within the striking circle. The ball is placed sixteen yards from the spot of the violation, or from where the ball went out of bounds.

The Striking Circle

The striking circle is actually a semicircle in the shape of the letter D. Because of its shape, the striking circle is also known as "the D."

The striking circle is the semicircle that is in the shape of the letter D.

In Case of a Tie

Field hockey is generally a low-scoring game though field hockey goals occur more frequently than goals in soccer. If there is a tie, then ten minutes of sudden death overtime is played, depending on the level or the league.

Players can try to make a goal only from within the striker's circle.

Unless it is a championship game, a high school game does not generally go into overtime. For a non-championship game, a tie score is acceptable. During sudden death, there is a ten-minute game of "seven a side." This is when seven players from each team, six fielders and the goalie, play for ten minutes, with regular game rules applying. The first team to score during sudden death wins. If no team scores, there is a five-minute break, after which

The goalkeeper is crucial during penalty shots as the responsibility
of saving the goal is solely his or hers.

the teams return for another ten-minute seven-a-side game. If there is still no score made in this time, the game switches to penalty score mode. Each team chooses five strokers, so called because of the penalty stroke they execute. The strokers go up against the opposing goalie one at a time and take a shot on the goal, each team alternating goalies every other shot. The team that scores first wins.

CHAPTER 4

The Defense and Offense

Field hockey is played by two teams of eleven members each on the field (ten players and one goalie). Two key aspects to team playing are communication and organization. Talking among teammates during a game is necessary for victory.

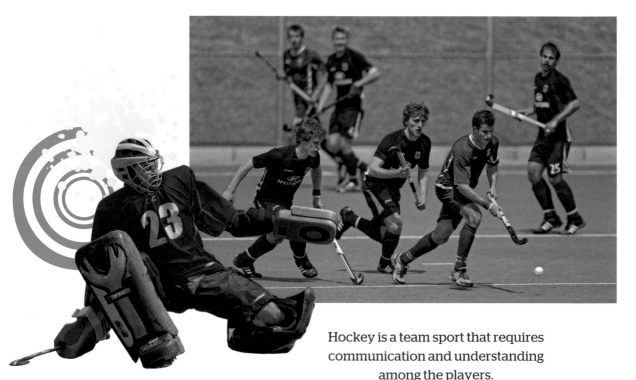

Hockey is a team sport that requires communication and understanding among the players.

Forwards

Nonverbal communication is also important. Eye contact and head nods, for example, are important when passing the ball and indicating where the ball should go. A player should know and understand the full duties not only of his or her own position, but of every other player on the field. Only then can a player make the right decisions during a game.

Forwards are the main offensive players of the team. There are three forwards on the front line, two inside forwards, and two wings. The forwards' task is to score a goal by invading the defense's area. Most of their work is carried out in the twenty-five-yard area of the opposing team. Whenever the ball is in this area, the offense has a chance of scoring. All of their efforts are put toward getting the ball into the striking circle and positioning it for a goal.

The offensive players (in blue) try to gain possession of the ball from the defense (in red) to make a goal.

The inside forwards stand in front of the goalie, positioning themselves to take a shot. They also try to block the goalie's view. The more they distract the goalie, the better the chances are for making a goal. The chief duty of the wings is to locate themselves in the zone in front of each goalpost. From this area, they can gain control of wide shots made on the goal, as well as following up on rebounds. Verbal communication is necessary in order for teammates to let each other know who has the best shot at the goal. Offensive forwards shout "Stroke!" to let other offensive linesmen know where they are, so the ball can be passed to them if they feel they have an opportunity to score.

Midfielders

Midfielders, being the only players that play all fifty yards of the field, are required to do a lot of running as they have the difficult task of playing both defense and offense. Midfielders are the offensive support for the forwards and need to stay close to the striking circle when the front line is attacking. When the opposing team is on the attack, midfielders must quickly recede and help the backs during defense.

Backs

The backs are the main defensive unit of the team. One of the main duties of a back is to "mark up." Marking up is the most intense and important defense in field hockey. It entails guarding the opposing forwards one on one. When the ball enters the twenty-five-yard defense area, every back must mark up the forward who is opposite them on the opposing team. The back needs to try his or her hardest to defend the goalie, since the forwards are constantly trying to obstruct a goalie's view and concentration.

The defensive players (in blue) rush to defend the goalie
as the offense (in red) attempts to score.

The sweeper and goalie are the last line of defense.
Communication between them is crucial to the game.

Goalie and Sweeper

The last line of defense against the opposing team is the goalie and the
sweeper. They work together to guard the goal. The goalie and sweeper
are the only defensive players who do not mark up, but because they are
centrally located at the end of the field, they have the best view of the game
playing out before them. This allows them to direct the rest of the defense,
calling out the numbers of offensive players who are not being marked up and
who pose a threat to the goal. A goalie's main duty is to block every shot, using
every part of his or her body to do so as long as he or she is within the striking
circle. The sweeper's duty is to cover any unguarded offensive player who
moves in toward the cage. Because the sweeper is the last defender before
the goal, he or she is often up against at least two unmarked offensive players
working together to score on the goal. This makes it important for the sweeper
and the goalie to constantly communicate with each other; the goalie judges
where to place his or her body to best protect the goal by knowing what moves
the sweeper plans to make.

Goalies can use any part of their body to prevent the ball from entering the goal, which is why they require so much protective gear.

Defensive Play

Defensive play starts even before the offense has positioned the ball in the striking circle. Defensive playing should begin the moment the opposing team gains control of the ball. At that point, every player, regardless of his

or her position, needs to think defensively to protect the goal and try to regain control of the ball. If players can't switch their thinking from offense to defense, they leave a weak spot for the opposing team to swoop in and score. Trying to recover the ball from the opposing team is as important an aspect of defensive play as guarding the goal.

Like all other sports, hockey has drills and plays that are practiced in order to perfect the play. Here, the Temple University's women's team practices before a match in Philadelphia.

To be a great field hockey player, it is important to have knowledge and understanding of the game beyond the physical requirements it takes. It is primarily a game of skill, stamina, and strength, but a player who thinks strategically will be able to solve problems, defend the goal, and maintain control of the ball. A good diet and lots of exercise are also vital for a player to get the most out of his or her game. Being both mentally and physically prepared is the best defensive strategy of all. And like anything else, the only way to improve is to practice, practice, practice.

Hockey is gaining worldwide popularity very quickly. Here, India plays against China at a competition in Thailand.

The Growing Popularity of Field Hockey

Field hockey continues to be embraced by more and more players around the world. Of the more than 200,000 people who play field hockey each year in the United States, 98 percent are students. In most schools and colleges, field hockey has become an integral part of the extracurricular program.

The National Collegiate Athletic Association (NCAA) began holding field hockey tournaments among different schools to crown a champion in the 1981. Old Dominion University in Norfolk, Virginia, dominated the NCAA championships during the first two decades, raking in a total of nine victories. Within the past few years, however, schools such as Wake Forest in North Carolina and the University of Maryland have been proving to be worthy competitors. In 2012, Princeton University won the championship for the first time. In 2013, the University of Connecticut returned to victory for the first time since 1985, true to the sport's long history in the Northeast.

The fact that teams who pose a threat to the championship title continue to pop up all over the country is a testament to the ever-growing popularity of the sport of field hockey. Today field hockey championships are played

India and Japan play against each other at the FIH Women's Field Hockey World Cup in Rosario, Argentina in 2010.

all over the world, with club championships, European championships, Asian games, Pan-American Games, and Inter-Continental Cup tournaments for qualification in the honored World Cup. The tournament for the most coveted international prize in hockey, the World Cup, is held every four years, with sixteen teams for men and sixteen teams for women competing for the title. Hockey is also played at the Olympics, which are held every four years, with the best players competing for their home country.

Field hockey was introduced in the Summer Olympics in 1908. China plays against Germany at the 2008 Summer Olympics held in Beijing.

The international appeal of the game makes the future of field hockey very promising, particularly for young American women. The NCAA currently has more than seventy-five Division I universities with active women's field hockey programs. Its popularity in the college circuit has managed to make field hockey a great source for college scholarship money.

The USFHA has set up a hall of fame based on the athletic achievement, long-term supremacy, innovation, and contributions to the sport for players and coaches in the United States. In order to qualify for the USFHA Hall of Fame, an individual must have been on his or her team for a minimum of five years. Anyone with a passion for the sport should be sure to visit the USFHA Hall of Fame at Ursinus College in Pennsylvania.

Glossary

advancing To push or move the ball without using the stick.

agility The gracefulness of a person who is quick and nimble.

apparel Clothing or things that are worn.

AstroTurf A synthetic, grass-like playing surface.

back stick To use the round, back side of a hockey stick to play the ball.

boycott To break commercial and social ties.

burgeoning Beginning to grow or flourish.

conventions The norm or the way something is usually done.

defense The team protecting the goal from the offense.

drive To hit the ball with a hard backswing.

Dyneema A man-made fiber that provides strength and absorption, yet is lightweight and flexible. It is used in making the field hockey stick.

encompass To completely surround.

hocquet The French term for a shepard's crook, from which hockey may be derived.

hook The head shape of the stick that hooks up in order to provide the maximum surface area for receiving and hitting the ball.

impromptu Done without planning or rehearsing.

jab To use the stick to take the ball away from an opponent.

Kevlar A man-made organic fiber that, like Dyneema, is used to strengthen the field hockey stick.

kilt A pleated skirt traditionally worn by Scotsmen, which today is part of most women's field hockey uniforms.

league An association of teams that plays competitive sports.

midi The head shape of the stick that is slightly longer than the shorti shape, with a larger hitting and stopping area.

offense The attacking team; the team trying to score a goal.

opponent A member of the opposite team.

passback Passing the ball to a teammate behind you at the beginning of a game.

pioneering Involving new ideas or methods.

prestigious Possessing a high status.

push pass A quick stroke of the stick using the wrist that executes an accurate pass.

reinforcement Something that strengthens.

retained Kept possession of.

scoop To hit the ball over the opponent's stick.

shorti The head shape of the stick carved from one piece of wood. This allows for quick maneuvering of the ball.

slap shot A powerful shot on the goal, made by using the back swing with hands slightly apart.

suffrage The right to vote.

undercutting To chop at the ball with the stick, lifting it in an unsafe way.

For More Information

Fédération Internationale de Hockey (FIH)
Avenue des Arts, 1 bte 5
1210 Bruxelles, Belgium
Website: http://www.fihockey.org

Field Hockey Federation, Inc.
2060 E. Avenida de los Arboles
D 479
Thousand Oaks, CA 91362
Website: http://www.socalfieldhockey.com/

Lead the Way, Inc.
P.O. Box 523
Saunderstown, RI 02874
(401) 269-9774
Website: http://www.leadthewayfieldhockey.com

National Collegiate Athletic Association (NCAA)
700 West Washington Street
P.O. Box 6222
Indianapolis, IN 46206
(317) 917-6222
Website: http://www.ncaa.org

National Federation of State High School Associations (NFHS)

P.O. Box 690

Indianapolis, IN 46206

Website: http://www.nfhs.org

National Field Hockey Coach's Association

P.O. Box 13289

Chandler AZ, 85248

Website: http://www.nfhca.org/

Potomac Field Hockey Inc.

43300-116 Southern Walk Plaza #611

Broadlands, VA 20148

(571) 210-0734

Website: http://www.potomacfieldhockey.org/

USA Field Hockey

One Olympic Plaza

Colorado Springs, CO 80909

(719) 866-4567

Website: http://www.teamusa.org/

Websites

Due to the changing nature of Internet links, the Rosen Publishing Group, Inc., has developed an online list of websites related to the subject of this book. This site is updated regularly. Please use this link to access the list:

http://www.rosenlinks.com/scc/fiho

For Further Reading

Anders, Elizabeth. *Field Hockey: Steps to Success—2nd Edition* (Steps to Success Sports Series). Champaign, IL: Human Kinetics, 2008.

Barth, Katrin. *Learning Field Hockey.* Aachen, Germany: Meyer and Meyer Verlag, 2007.

Johnson-Crell, Erica. *Mastering the Net: Field Hockey Goalkeeping Basics.* Terre Haute, IN: Wish Publishing, 2007.

Lewis Swope, Bob. *Youth Field Hockey Drills, Strategies, Plays and Games Handbook.* St. Louis, MO: Jacobob Press LLC, 2011.

Powell, Jane. *Hockey: Skills. Techniques. Tactics* (Crowood Sports Guides). Wiltshire, SN: Crowood, 2012.

Walter, Ryan. *Hockey Plays and Strategies.* Champaign, IL: Human Kinetics, 2009.

Bibliography

Anders, Elizabeth, and Sue Myers. *Field Hockey: Steps to Success.* Champaign, IL: Human Kinetics, 1998.

Connolly, Helen. *Field Hockey: Rules, Tips, Strategy, and Safety.* New York, NY: Rosen Publishing Group, 2005.

Hurtig, Jennifer. *Field Hockey.* New York, NY: AV2 by Weigl, 2014.

Maloney, Christopher. *Field Hockey: Understanding the Game 2014-15.* North Charleston, SC: CreateSpace, 2013.

Swissler, Becky, and Tracey Belbin. *Winning Field Hockey for Girls.* New York, NY: Facts on File, 2003.

Index

Index

About the Authors

Helen Connolly is a writer who lives in Brooklyn, New York.

Abigael McIntyre is a writer who enjoys most sports, including volleyball and field hockey, but especially those played in the great outdoors. When she's not writing or reading, she enjoys hiking and backpacking in Montana's Beartooth Mountains.

Photo Credits

The photographs in this book are used by permission and through the courtesy of: Cover photo Getty Images, 1; Back Cover: File Upload Bot (Magnus Manske)/ commons.wikimedia.org; © DeanHarty/shutterstock.com; © Micha Klootwijk/ shutterstock.com; © Baronb/shutterstock.com; © Tomas Fritz/shutterstock. com; © aquariagirl1970/shutterstock.com; © Haslam Photography/ shutterstock.com; © Micha Klootwijk/shutterstock.com, 1, 8, 28; © DeanHarty/ shutterstock.com, 1, 8, 28; © Han borg/commons.wikimedia.org, 2; © Rec79/ commons.wikimedia.org, 2; © mooinblack/shutterstock.com, 5, 18, 24, 33, 37; © almonfoto/shutterstock.com, 5; © Voyager/commons.wikimedia.org, 6; © Gobonobo/commons.wikimedia.org, 7; © Cliftonian/Vitaliy Saveliev/ Виталий Савельев, 8; © Epsilon 42/commons.wikimedia.org, 9; © Tony Alter/ commons.wikimedia.org, 10, 11; © Aspen Photo/shutterstock.com, 12, 15, 36; © imagedb.com/shutterstock.com, 12; © Fma12/commons.wikimedia.org, 13; © Frtzw906/commons.wikimedia.org, 14; © Jürgen-Michael Glubrecht/ commons.wikimedia.org, 16; © Alexander Kalina/shutterstock.com, 17, 29, 31, 32; © NilsKruse/commons.wikimedia.org, 17; © Racheal Grazias/shutterstock. com, 19; © BlackIceNRW/commons.wikimedia.org, 21; © Willem van de Kerkhof/shutterstock.com, 22, 28; © Steve Lovegrove/shutterstock.com, 22; © Corepics VOF/shutterstock.com, 23, 27; © Maxisport/shutterstock.com, 25 © manzrussali/shutterstock.com, 26, 34,35; © Prixel Creative/shutterstock.com, 28; © EcoPrint/shutterstock.com, 30; © Luis Oviedo Ortiz/commons.wikimedia. org, 38; © Flickr upload bot/commons.wikimedia.org, 39.